STUDENT-ATHLETES:
EQUIPPED FOR LIFE

RONNIE MASON

Copyright © 2023 by Ronnie Mason.

Produced for publication by
The Author's Pen, LLC
PO Box 16314
Fort Worth, Texas 76162
www.tapwriting.com

ALL RIGHTS ARE RESERVED.
No part of this publication may be reproduced, stored in a retrieval system, or transmitted, in any form or by any means, electronic, technical, photocopying, recording or otherwise, without the prior written permission of the publisher.

Scriptures taken from the Holy Bible, New International Version®, NIV®. Copyright © 1973, 1978, 1984, 2011 by Biblica, Inc.™ Used by permission of Zondervan. All rights reserved worldwide. www.zondervan.com The "NIV" and "New International Version" are trademarks registered in the United States Patent and Trademark Office by Biblica, Inc.™

Student-Athletes: Equipped for Life

1st paperback ed. ISBN 978-1-948248-53-2

www.ingramcontent.com/pod-product-compliance
Lightning Source LLC
Chambersburg PA
CBHW041132110526
44592CB00020B/2777

Up until 16, he was a 3-sport athlete—bowling, football, and basketball. By 11th grade, his high school football coach made him aware of his potential and praised his athletic abilities. That was enough to propel him to become a football college scholarship recipient at Coastal Carolina University.

Coach Ronnie Mason was a 2-time all-conference performer. He came close to achieving his dreams of playing in the NFL, but it wasn't in His will. Since his pursuit came to an end, he has been coaching and training athletes from NC to FL since 2013.

In 2014, he turned his passion into a business: The Solution Dynamics (TSD aka TSDATHLETES). Since its inception, it has developed into a Nonprofit organization (TSDARC) that has a little league football organization attached called the TSD Bears known for "*Providing a Solution for a Dynamic Future.*"

Coach Ronnie Mason is a loving husband and the father of 3 boys. He strives to lead a life worth living, and create a legacy so their reign will be legendary.

Forever a product of Durham, NC. Ronnie Mason is the oldest of five children, and was raised by his mother and grandmother. His roots in sports and faith stem from his grandmother who is a die-hard MJ and Lebron fan, and currently, an avid bowler.

His first sport was bowling. It's one of those things that teach you correction, and requires poise and consistency.

He fell in love with all sports by the age of 10. He had the ability but not the resources. At age 12, he played for his uncle's on a basketball team. That was where he first learned he was gifted. Then, he became a 2-sport athlete.

At 13, he found out about politics in sports but I played for a coach who visited his home, and begged his mom to allow him to play for his basketball team.

Knowledge and experience are the cheat codes of life. Choosing to gain knowledge from a book, a coach, or a mentor, you are ahead of the game.

    Go Get 'Em

    Sincerely,

    COACH MASON

EPILOGUE

I want to thank you for your support in reading this book. The journey has just begun. I hope you've been reminded of your passion and purpose.

On your journey as a student-athlete, embrace being a student. The phrase, "you learn something new every day," keeps you in that seat.

Evolution is development, and evolving is about growing and learning in the process. I want to make sure you are prepared and that you embrace the grind ahead of you because you are prepared to go get whatever your heart desires.

Within the pages of this book, I've expressed the following life lessons to help you achieve greatness: knowledge from your education, belonging to a family or team, the ability to multitask and juggle responsibility, your understanding of what's important, and staying humble.

I am proud of you already. First, you are choosing to be on the team instead of being in a gang. Second, you are reading instead of playing a game.

"The hardest skill to acquire in this sport is the one where you compete all out, give it all you have, and you are still getting beat no matter what you do. When you have the killer instinct to fight through that, it is very special."

Eddie Reese

Student-Athletes: Equipped for Life

same kind of hard work by watching films, taking care of the classroom, asking the right question about the playbook, and getting stronger in the weight room (if your next chapter is in football).

Be sure to continue putting in the work that's required, watching the market, taking care of things at work, being prepared to answer questions, and always getting better in your new role. I know if anybody can do that thing, that job, or handle that responsibility, it will be you because you are equipped for the journey called life.

Go, get ready for practice.

don't get back, so don't waste it. Make sure it was worth it in the long run.

The celebration and appreciation go to you on graduation day. The last thing you want is to lose on this night. Going out like that would be devastating and weird. If you do happen to lose, know that you aren't a loser. You are an achiever, goal-oriented, focused, hardworking individual. Any team or business would love to have someone with those attributes. When they give you that chance, you already possess knowledge that no one can take from you. You belong to something bigger and better than where you were before, though it will be different. You can handle anything they throw at you, especially if you love what you're doing and why you do it. Your values and morals will keep you on track to achieve success and do what needs to be done. And because you waited your turn and you remember how tough it was to show that you deserve a shot, humility won't be an issue at all. Those positions or tryouts that you desire after college won't be given to you. You have to GO GET 'EM..

You deserve to go get everything your heart desires. You are built to overcome and endure the journey unless you are a quitter, and based on your current resume of being an athlete, you are not a quitter. Just make sure that as your next chapter takes shape, you focus on continuing to put in the

This moment is bittersweet. You made it, you stuck with it. You completed the task, you overcame, you persevered, and you kept your position and job. The appreciation for a job well done is today, but it's coming to an end. You have done so much to be in this position. You practiced day in and day out, you worked out all year, you had meetings, you had class, studies, and exams. You balanced it all while staying out of trouble and keeping your eyes on the prize. Sometimes, you chose priorities over fun and responsibilities over experiences. You did it. Now the last game is here, and you want to go out with a bang, so go make plays.

You have been given an opportunity to showcase your talent. That is an accomplishment on its own. There are people in this world who would die for such a moment. You deserve a pat on the back, but you may not get that from your family until graduation day. They don't understand the blood, sweat, and tears that you put in. After college, you will get another chance to play, hopefully. But if not, that is ok. Why? When you graduate you put yourself in conversation or consideration for opportunities in a certain line of work. I want to make you aware of one thing: make sure what you study is a line of work in which you're genuinely interested. Make sure it's something you're passionate about. Don't waste time majoring in something that has an easy road or your someone else prefer you take. Time is something you

PRACTICE #11

GRADUATION

"Goals on the road to achievement cannot be achieved without discipline and consistency."
Denzel Washington

So if you stay ready, you ain't gotta get ready, and that is how I run my life."

Will Smith

Student-Athletes: Equipped for Life

asking the right question about the playbook, and getting stronger in the weight room.

Consistency is important in the game, and in life. You will have to remain consistent with a lot of things. Going to work, taking care of your mind, body, and one day, somebody else. You may have a wife that you have to keep happy consistently, and kids you have to feed and take care of consistently, no matter what's going on.

You did what you were supposed to do, you were ready. You heard your name called several times on the intercom. You were praised by your teammates, and your coach even said he knew you had it in you. He is proud of you. Don't take any of it for granted. Take every play, every day, every opportunity, and every game, and make the best of it. Don't take any plays off. Continue to put in extra work because it's promising. If you continue to work your tail off, there will be a chance for you to have a successful career in college. If you take these same practices into life, you will be successful in everything you do.

Go, get ready for practice.

moment to demonstrate that you've been putting in extra work, watching extra film, taking care of your responsibilities in the classroom, asking the right questions about the playbook, and getting stronger in the weight room.

Imagine this scenario.

Game 1 came, and you saw some action on special teams. Your family came to see you play and be the guy from high school catching the ball, sacking QBs, throwing touchdowns, flying around, making plays on the ball, or scoring touchdowns. That was then, and this is now. This is your new reality, and no one is experiencing it except you. But remember to be patient and stick to all the steps you took to prepare for game 1.

Game 2 is here and the guy ahead of you just tapped his helmet and the coach chose to go with the other guy who has been in the program, knows the playbook, made some plays last season, and put in some hours to deserve what you want. This represents an opportunity. This means your number is being called next.

Game 3. An injury occurs and your number is called. "Come on, Son, show me what you got," says your position coach.

Let's hope you were still doing everything consistently up to this point—putting in extra work, watching extra film, taking care of the classroom,

t's game time. How was that scrimmage? Were you prepared for it during camp? Were you a deer in headlights? Was the moment too big for you? Was your name called and did you make the play?

Just know that it may not have been enough. From this moment forward, understand that everything is politicized. All the boxes have to be checked for you to be that #1 guy. Looking on the bright side of things, if you did everything right in the scrimmage, you have started a good campaign for yourself. By the next practice, you could now be #2 on the depth chart. One of the good things about football is there's always a next-man-up opportunity, so stay ready and keep working.

The game is here; the game is now. You are on the sidelines, ready and patiently waiting. Developing patience is so important because waiting can be frustrating, especially when you know you are ready. But accept it, tolerate the delay, and suffer without getting angry or upset. Why? Because in life, you will discover that you do not control anything but your attitude and your efforts. In the words of the late Nipsey Hussle, *"How long should I stay dedicated? How long until opportunity meets preparation?"* When your time is called, you have to show up and show out. When that opportunity presents itself, you have to take advantage of it. When the politics don't affect the decision that's being made and the stars aligned, it's your time to be that guy. It's your

49

PRACTICE #10

GAME TIME

"I never left the field saying I could have done more to get ready and that gives me peace of mind."
Peyton Manning

"Sometimes you need to feel the pain and sting of defeat to activate the real passion and purpose that God predestined inside of you."
Chadwick Boseman

Student-Athletes: Equipped for Life

Student-Athletes: Equipped for Life

magnitude. Then, there's practice. Hopefully, you made it to lunch and weren't too tired from your morning. Practice is normally scheduled in the middle of the day, which is good because you got the rest of the day to finish your obligations as a student-athlete. That might look like studying, putting in extra work to get ahead of your competition (teammate or opposition), watching a film, participating in study groups, tutoring, or relieving stress. Make sure you get it all done because all of these things matter if you aspire to prove that you belong and that you deserve a shot during this scrimmage.

The scrimmage is similar to an audition. You know your role, you take the right steps, and you perform when your card is called. Let's just hope you nail the audition. If you can get the part and handle everything thrown your way, including the pressure the coaches put on you and the expectations they had when they chose you, I think you are deserving. There's a good chance you have earned the opportunity to showcase your talents in the game.

Go, get ready for practice.

Student-Athletes: Equipped for Life

My goal is to motivate you as athletes and nurture your aspirations to continue the game, up to the collegiate level and pro. I want you to be prepared for what's ahead. And yes, little league and middle school athletes have their tough days, too. During the tough days, always remember why you play—it's fun, your parents have encouraged you, the structure, your friends, and your sense of belonging.

Your schedule is as follows: your parents wake you up for school. School is from 8 am - 3 pm, which is all in one setting. You may have a study hall, but normally practice right after school. Then, you go home to a meal prepared by your mom or guardian without a worry (unless your situation is unfortunate). Then, you get reminded to do your homework if you didn't complete your assignments during class. But by 8 pm, you are done and ready to get on the video game before bed. This is a typical day in the life of a student-athlete. Must be nice, and trust me, it is.

In college, the grind changes. The responsibilities and the disciplines fall on you. It's all up to you. Going to class, eating well, showing up on time, doing your homework, and keeping up with your grades and studies.

As a college athlete, you may have workouts first thing in the morning at 5 am or 6 am (depending on the part of the year). Then, you may have two or three classes each day, a position meeting that you better not miss, and a team meeting of the same

Finally, it is time to show what you possess, how much better you've gotten, how much faster you are, and how much stronger you've become. It's time to demonstrate that you have learned the playbook and show that you are ready for an opportunity to prove yourself.

In sports, we are lucky we get to practice over and over again before facing an opponent. You can watch last year's footage of what that team did well, what they struggled with, and how they handled pressure and dealt with adversity. But then there is the reality of whether you are prepared and ready to accept the challenge. You will have to go against people that know your weaknesses, your strengths, and how to expose you.

So how do you approach this dilemma? You don't! Just know that this scrimmage is to give you experience, prepare you for tough opponents, and give you a chance to see what you should work on before week 1.

Would you believe that football or the journey of a student-athlete is a scrimmage for real life? In many ways, it prepares you for life experiences like adversity, trials, and tough situations. In football and other sports, you have adversity, competition, and tough opponents. Luckily for all athletes, especially young athletes, you don't have the same level of requirements as a collegiate or professional player.

PRACTICE #9

LIVE CONTACT/SCRIMMAGE

"I hated every minute of training, but I said, don't quit. Suffer now and live the rest of your life a champion."
Muhammad Ali

go, come on. Your words can bring life or they can burn bridges. Be conscious. Think before you speak, and realize your coaches will always be right. And trust me, there will be plenty of times when you will have to bite your mouthpiece to avoid getting into trouble.

So, if the coach tells you that you aren't starting, you're not going to be in the rotation, or you're not ready, accept it and do something about it.

Go, get ready for practice.

"Don't take it personal. Make it personal."
Coach Ronnie Mason

qualities, and achievements. Just like your boss or teacher. Your words have a lot of power.

The power of the tongue started in a religious setting. There was a time I had an issue with a coach. At the time, I didn't respect him because he never played in my position. His approach wasn't genuine. He always singled me out for my mistakes, but I never disrespected him. However, I did voice my opinion, which affected my playing time. Why? Like in business, the customer is always right. In this case, the coach is always going to win.

Back to the power of the tongue and speaking things into existence. At that time, I didn't know I was one of Coastal Carolina University's biggest recruits in terms of size and talent in 2005. I wasn't in the starting lineup when the season began. By game 3, I wished I had chosen another school, but I prayed for an opportunity before I really understood prayer and the power of that statement.

By game week 4, someone got hurt. I cracked the lineup. Although I wasn't happy about my teammate getting hurt, I was glad to get an opportunity. A opened a door for me that day, and there was no going back

I want you to understand that you have to speak life daily. Make declarations daily, and when that weight on the bench press is the most you have ever done, you have to tap in and declare, *I've got this, let's*

Now that you have your equipment on, don't forget your mouthpiece. This reminds me of sayings I heard growing up. Perhaps you've heard some of these, too.

"Be careful what you ask for."

"You'd better watch your mouth."

"Who you think you're talking to?"

"Keep on, and somebody is going to pop you right in the mouth."

"Your mouth is going to get you in trouble."

The good thing about having a mouthpiece on is that it limits what comes out. You have the same message no matter what.

On the other hand, the person you are speaking to may not be able to fully understand the call, checks, or strengths. The message has to be delivered before the ball is snapped so that everyone is on the same page.

In your daily life off the field, sometimes you and your teacher, you and your parents, or you and your boss may not be on the same page. As a student-athlete, sometimes you and your coach won't be on the same page, but that doesn't give you the privilege or right to express yourself recklessly. Put that mouthpiece back on, bite it, and swallow those words. No, your coach isn't your parent, but they have earned your respect because of their abilities,

PRACTICE #8

THE MOUTHPIECE

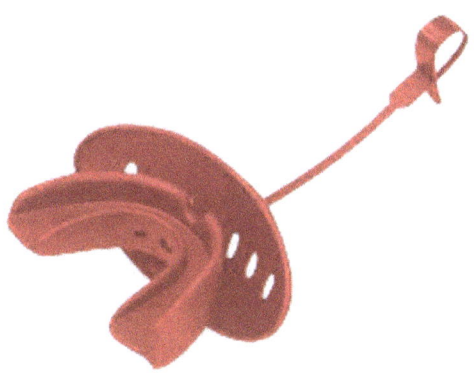

"Winning is a habit. Watch your thoughts, they become your beliefs. Watch your beliefs, they become your words. Watch your words, they become your actions. Watch your actions, they become your habits. Watch your habits, they become your character."
Vince Lombardi

Student-Athletes: Equipped for Life

slip up on your grades and start slacking. It shows in your work ethic and difficulty with receiving constructive criticism.

Don't lose your footing, keep pushing forward. Don't just do it once, do it again and again with an attitude of, *I still have work to do*. Know that you aren't done yet. There is still much work to do. The phrase *ten toes down* comes to mind, which means I'm still me, I'm still here. I am solid, devoted, and committed. Your journey can keep you humble or humble you.

In football, every position has a stance. It shows that your feet are a good distance apart to ensure you're ready. Ready to take advantage of every day, every opponent, and every obstacle?

In summary, stay grounded, stay *ten toes down*, keep pushing forward, and keep your cleat game right!

Go, get ready for practice.

"I am always asked, what's the secret to success? But there are no secrets. Be humble, be hungry. And always be the hardest worker in the room."
Dwayne Johnson

Listen, we all know as athletes how important the shoe game is. The brand you rock, the colors, and how it flows with your uniform. A person is often judged on his/her appearance and it's normally from head to toe. As a normal person, your shoes may complement your outfit, but in sports, your footwear also enhances your performance.

As student-athletes, getting compliments on your performance and having the crowd cheering you on is so fulfilling. The first time you hear your name over the intercom after making a play during a game, or getting your first award on stage for an athletic achievement, your support system celebrates you.

Success could come from having on the right shoes or cleats that give you good grip and traction.

Can you imagine? The shoes are lighter so you were faster. You looked good, and you played well. They were comfortable, and you just felt like a million bucks. At the end of the day, it wasn't just you. So, for those achievements, or that game, or that season that was groundbreaking and eye-opening to the spectators, remember to stay grounded, stay diligent, stay humble, and stay hungry. There is a phrase that we have used in the past: *Stay hungry and stay humble.*

Cleats are designed to make sure you have good footing and to minimize slip-ups. The easiest way to show you have lost your humble ways would be to

PRACTICE #7

THE CLEATS

"One man be a crucial ingredient on a team, but one man cannot make a team."
Kareem Abdul-Jabbar

Student-Athletes: Equipped for Life

and how the world sees you. Just as if someone in the world caught you off guard or doing something you'd be ashamed of later. That level of value should go into your decision-making. Always think about what you would lose if someone caught you doing something that questions the knowledge you possess, embarrasses the name on the jersey, and waste all that time you spent handling and balancing your responsibilities. Don't get caught with your pants down.

Go, get ready for practice.

> *"Not wanting to disappoint is what pushed me to be successful."*
> **Jerry Rice**

When you get up in the morning and get dressed, one of the first things you grab are your pants. Why? Because your prized possessions and values are covered. This applies to the game of football, too. Those padded pants are there to protect valuable assets.

Values alongside your morals are the focal point of this practice. Since you were a kid, people around you that cared about your well-being have tried teaching you right from wrong. Morals are the standard of behavior or beliefs. It determines what is and is not acceptable to you. For example, walking out of the house or into a store with no pants on is not acceptable. On certain levels of football, if you don't have your pads on correctly or placed properly, you will be told to leave the game. It's not punishment. The referees value your safety and well-being.

The reason you play the game or sport of your choosing is because you see value in doing so. You may find it fun, interesting, competitive, or you value it as an outlet or opportunity to change your circumstance. Any of these reasons will keep you on the straight and narrow. Choosing to do wrong, getting kicked off the team, or not being able to play is usually a reflection of your decisions and moral compass.

As a student-athlete, making the right decisions should be important because you value the outcome

PRACTICE #6

THE PANTS/GIRDLE

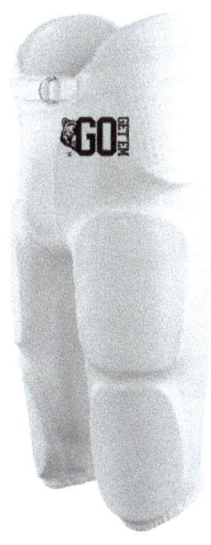

"I've always made a total effort, even when the odds seemed entirely against me. I never quit trying; I never felt that I didn't have a chance to win."

Arnold Palmer

you become good men and women, ultimately. And in being good people, you also become good spouses and parents, too.

Handle what you can handle and know that your hustle creates your income. This means that hard work pays off. So put on your gloves and get to work.

Go, get ready for practice.

"I have a responsibility to lead, in more ways than one, and I take that very seriously."
Lebron James

Some players can't play the game well anymore without gloves. The technology, the grip, and the protective measures designed for your hands and for securing the football have become necessary for athletes to play at a high level.

One thing has been overlooked, and that's multitasking. When it comes to athletes, whether little league or professional, we often forget to consider the need for athletes to develop multi-tasking skills, and simply learning to manage busier lives.

You have to be a student to remain a *student-athlete*. You have your schedule, practice, workouts, meetings, socializing, travel, entertainment, and games while maintaining your academic requirements such as homework, studying, exams, tests, and internships. The beauty is that once you get the hang of it and you can finally start tolerating the pain, you will persevere.

As you continue to age and experience life, you will find yourself having to handle and juggle more than one thing. For example, when you become a spouse and then a parent, you have sleepless nights only to get up and go to work. Then, you try to find time to manage your work-life balance. Don't forget about giving time to your spouse and the house. My coaches have always stated that this isn't just about the sport. Your coaching team is trying to make sure

On this journey, the things you have to deal with and manage could be big or small. It's your responsibility to handle them. You're the one who has to make the tough decisions to prioritize, scale, and balance your life. Don't be scared of this knowledge—you are equipped for this. The life to come isn't going to be easy, but you can handle it by grasping concepts and managing them.

The gloves worn by athletes help make the game a little easier. Here are a few examples of sports that include gloves as part of the standard equipment.

Boxing

Boxing gloves protect your hands and wrists. They are also easier on your face and body.

Soccer

The goalie wears gloves to protect the hands as they constantly have to deflect balls coming at full speed.

Baseball

Baseball gloves make the leather-wrapped brick, the baseball, catchable no matter how fast it's moving.

Football

Football gloves are designed to help with gripping, securing, blocking, and catching.

PRACTICE #5

THE GLOVES

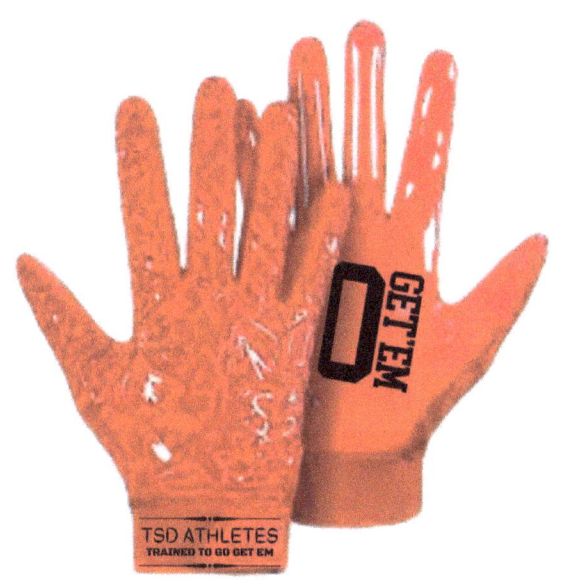

"The price of greatness is responsibility."
Winston Churchill

Student-Athletes: Equipped for Life

matter. Sports changed my narrative a lot. Why? Instead of having no purpose or just wasting time, I had practice at a set time every day of every week, which is what adults have to do every day—go put in work in the company they work for for a set time multiple days a week. But then some felt gang life was where they belonged, or they didn't have the skills to play sports or hated being told what to do so they just ran the streets doing what they wanted to do. The downside of that scenario is that there are only a couple of different outcomes on the streets, and when that one outcome leads to a funeral, it is hard on the people you belong to.

You have to realize that you're representing family and not just any family, but your family. Good, bad, or indifferent, it's your family, and you'll likely have to plan and then deliver or make a big play for the family. They need you, may depend on you, or have big expectations for you as you endure this journey.

Go, get ready for practice.

"A team is where a boy can prove his courage on his own. A gang is where a coward goes to hide."
Mickey Mantle

The movie, "*Remember the Titans*" is a must-see film if you love football or Denzel Washington. In the movie, there's a scene where two of the characters have an exchange we can learn from.

Julius, argued with Bertier during camp and said, "I'm supposed to wear myself out for the team. What team? Nah, what I'm going to do is I'm going to look out for myself and I'm going to get mine." Bertier's response was, "See, man, that is the worst attitude I have ever heard." Julius rebutted and stated, "Attitude reflects leadership, Captain!" That moment in the movie was significant for two reasons. One, the jersey you wear is important because it shows you are a part of a team or belong to an organization. And when I say belong to, technically I'm referencing ownership or slavery. They have rights to you, own your schedule, what you wear, and can place certain restrictions at any moment, especially in collegiate and professional settings. The second way you can view that is the name on the back of that jersey.

Team sports or sports, in general, have prevented harm from befalling kids who would rather partake in sports than stay on the street corner over the endzone. They prefer to make a deal than score a bucket or a touchdown. Being on a team can keep you safe. It gives you a sense of belonging because you have a team that is almost like family to you. You belong to something bigger than you, but you

PRACTICE #4

THE JERSEY

"To know that you can navigate the wilderness on your own—to know that you can stay true to your beliefs, trust yourself, and survive it—that is true belonging."
Brene Brown

Student-Athletes: Equipped for Life

- Be smart about what you put in your body.
- Be smart about what deals you accept and what team you choose.

Go, get ready for practice.

"If you take the knowledge out of my head and take the experiences that I have, I'm broke, I'm nothing."
Eric Thomas

athlete prepares you for these moments. Game planning is preparation, practice is preparation, and studying as a student-athlete makes you smarter, and ultimately, puts you in position to GO GET 'EM.

The helmet is for the head, and as you continue to experience life, you will hear things like:

- *A mind is a terrible thing to waste.*
- *It's mental.*
- *You can overcome anything you put your mind to.*

The brain, which the helmet protects, controls your ability to think, talk, feel, see, hear, remember things, walk, and much more. If your head is not in the game, your body will follow.

> *"Follow your passion, figure out what that may be before it's too late."*
> **Steve Harvey, *"Act like a Success, Think Like a Success"***

Your gift is the vehicle that helps you navigate your life after sports. I hope you make it to pro, but while in that seat, you have to use your head much more. Be smart.

- Be smart about the decisions you make because they can be costly.
- Be smart when it comes to your finances and how you invest.

In your lifetime, you may have heard the saying, "If his head wasn't connected to his body, he would lose that, too."

In football (full padded), you can not take part in the game without your helmet, nor can you contribute to the outcome. You should be able to retain information, be teachable, crave smartness, and have a passion for getting better. And one of the only ways to get better is to learn from your mistakes. If not, learn the process of doing so. Getting better, getting smarter, keeping your head in the game, focusing, preparing, developing, and executing the game plan all make you a successful athlete. And success on the field prepares you for success after the game.

These are things you have to do to go far in the game or the sport of your liking, be a starter, win a spot on the roster, make all conferences, or get that scholarship. You will have to GO GET 'EM. You have to retain information and be able to execute plays when they're called. For example, when it is time to step up and make a key block, catch, run, or tackle. To be in the moment, you have to keep your head in the game.

Looking ahead, one day will be an ex-athlete, father, mother, or someone's spouse, and there will be times when you have to remain focused, keep your head in the game of life, and make that play for your family. The experience you gain from being an

PRACTICE #3

THE HELMET

"Wisdom is always an overmatch for strength."
Phil Jackson

Student-Athletes: Equipped for Life

Student-Athletes: Equipped for Life

When competing in football, certain requirements are part of the uniform. You have things like cleats to give you a fair shot or opportunity and then accessories to give you a little bit of SWAG (real-world talk)!

Equipment List

Helmet

Jersey

Gloves

Padded Girdle

Knee pads

Cleats

Mouthpiece

As you continue to read, I will explain the importance of each piece of equipment, and why it is being used, what it is designed to protect, and the benefits of adhering to these requirements as a student-athlete. But first, I want you to recognize the value you bring to the table, your strengths and your attributes, and apply them so you can make the life you envision for yourself a reality. This is my prayer for you, Jesus' name. Amen!

Go, get ready for practice.

> *"It's not pressure unless you are not prepared."*
> **Colin Kaepernick**

Most coaches have a belief system or code of ethics in which they live by whether they are raised Christian, Catholic, or Muslim. I believe in Jesus and the rest of the Holy Trinity. The Bible talks about the "whole armor of God" being comprised of:

- The helmet of *Salvation*,
- The breastplate of *Righteousness*,
- The shield of faith,
- The loins girded with truth,
- The sword of the *Spirit*, and
- The shoes of peace.

There are only two sports that have this much equipment and one of them is, you guessed it, **football**.

Every sport has a dress code or PPE requirement, similar to what you'd expect when working on a job in America. Your uniform requirements have a specific purpose:

1. To make sure you look the part (professional or uniformed).
2. To demonstrate unity (that you belong).
3. To protect you from harm.

PRACTICE #2

WHAT KIND OF EQUIPMENT IS REQUIRED?

*"For we are God's handiwork,
created in Christ Jesus to do good works,
which God prepared in advance for us to do."*
(Ephesians 2:10 NIV)

Student-Athletes: Equipped for Life

"A smooth sea never made a skilled sailor."
Franklin D Roosevelt

Be responsible

Be responsible because you are now doing things that most don't, and therefore, your responsibilities are more than average. What may be free time for others, becomes your grind time, your practice time, and your new homework time. You are in season when they have finished with theirs. You have events scheduled all day within an athletics program. And while enduring all of that, you are still managing your time and seeing results.

Be goal driven

You know your why. You have a reason. You get to decide to follow *God's plan* (Drizzy). You have MVP goals, All-American goals, All-Conference goals, and All-Area goals in the sports world. You strive for making the dean's list, A honor roll, A&B honor roll, and degrees.

The sport you fall in love with is fun. Never forget that! Once the fun stops, it is time to step away.

Go, get ready for practice!

While choosing to be a student-athlete or a sportsperson, here are lessons to learn on your journey.

Lessons for *Student-Athletes*

Be coachable

Be willing to listen to criticism, and apply it.

Be disciplined

If you want results, keep working. And work with integrity.

Keep a winning attitude and a fighting spirit

Don't be a quitter even if it is up to you. Sometimes, in sports, you have to throw in the towel (sports dialogue), but you are fighting for victory.

Develop a competitive nature

You want to win, you like incentives, you like accolades, you are *'bout that life* (real-world talk). To win, you have to go for it.

Make the effort and put in the hard work

Choosing to be an athlete requires a lot from you. You have to sweat, put in the work, and do things others won't. You practice and study every day on the way to playing professionally.

Some people have a love for the game, some develop an interest on their own, while others are guided to the sport by parents or a guardian. Most athletes who decide to go down the road of sports learn valuable life lessons. These lessons prepare you for the real world, real life, adversity, ups and downs, losses, and pain. It's an *athlete* thing.

It was all worth it will likely be the sentiment of 70% or more of current and ex-athletes alike because of the thrill, the experience, the fun, and the memories afforded by playing the game.

Some people might believe you receive special treatment, some may hate your accomplishments, some might appear as if they want you to lose, some may even want to be like you, while others may want to knock your block off (football lingo) or take you out of the game. But once again, *It was all worth it.*

You can do so much with this opportunity. Some athletes take advantage of the situation, some take it for granted, some blow it, while some just don't know how or what to be paying attention to.

I've written this book for those who believe they've missed the opportunity. It's never too late to make the game-changing play (sports dialogue), and that applies both on and off the field.

PRACTICE #1

WHY CHOOSE TO BE A STUDENT-ATHLETE?

"Do you know what my favorite part of the game is? The opportunity to play."
Mike Singletary

capable of surviving workouts that are meant to break you? Highly unlikely.

But you are! So get ready for practice. We have a lot to go over; new plays to introduce, and the game plan for those of you that are dressing this week. Let's GO GET 'EM!

INTRODUCTION

Allow me to paint a picture for you using the *Picasso Theory*. You put yourself through so much to be in your shoes or cleats. You have experienced days when quitting was a thought, but never in question. You have seen friends have fun while you had practice, meetings, film sessions, or an away game. Sometimes, you asked yourself, *why am I doing this*?

The question should be, what can I learn from this experience? Is it worth it? And, that's why this book is being presented to you. I want you to understand the attributes, the mentality you have, the values you possess, and lastly, what you are capable of once the game ends for you.

Like everything else, you can choose to make the most of the opportunity. And you best believe, it's a blessing and privilege to be on the team and a part of the journey.

A lot of people would love to be in your shoes. Some people feel they can do it, as well. But, are they built like that? Are they about that life? Are they

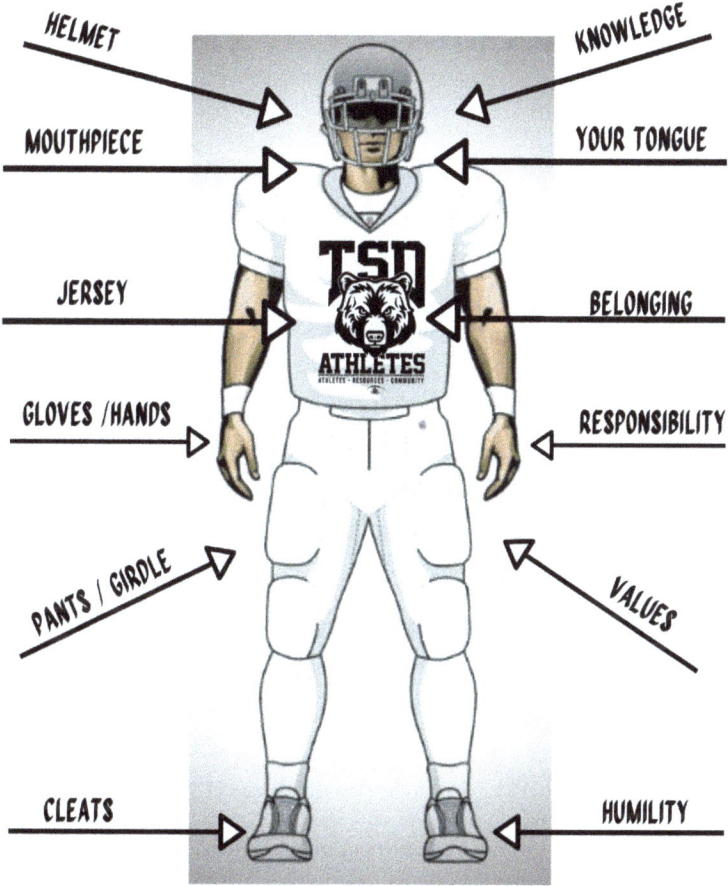

TABLE OF CONTENTS

Introduction 5
Practice #1 : Why Choose to be a Student-Athlete? 8
Practice #2 : What Kind of Equipment is Required? 14
Practice #3 : The Helmet 18
Practice #4 : The Jersey 22
Practice #5 : The Gloves 26
Practice #6 : The Pants/Girdle 30
Practice #7 : The Cleats 34
Practice #8 : The Mouthpiece 38
Practice #9 : Live Contact/Scrimmage 42
Practice #10 : Game Time 48
Practice #11 : Graduation 54
Epilogue 61